MILITARY MEDALS, DECORATIONS & ORDERS
Robert W.D. Ball & Paul Peters

MILITARY MEDALS, DECORATIONS & ORDERS

OF THE UNITED STATES & EUROPE

A Photographic Study
to the Beginning of World War II

Robert W.D. Ball & Paul Peters

Schiffer Military/Aviation History
Atglen, PA

Book Design by Bonnie Hensley.

Copyright © 1994 by Robert W.D. Ball & Paul Peters.
Library of Congress Catalog Number: 93-87476

Printed in China.
ISBN: 0-88740-579-7

We are interested in hearing from authors with book ideas on related topics.

Published by Schiffer Publishing Ltd.
77 Lower Valley Road
Atglen, PA 19310
Please write for a free catalog.
This book may be purchased from the publisher.
Please include $2.95 postage.
Try your bookstore first.

Contents

Acknowledgements

This book is due in large part to the unstinting sharing of information and assistance given by a large number of collectors and dealers of medals, orders and decorations, as well as the necessary support of our families at all times – thank God for their understanding and patience!

Our deep thanks to William J. Murray, Jr. of Connecticut, whose camera equipment, guidance and continual help made the task of getting all this material on film infinitely easier!

In many ways, the following members of OMSA and/or ASMIC, as well as individual collectors, have made our job of identification, evaluation and description of pieces shown on these pages a joy rather than a chore. To all of you, our heartfelt appreciation.

Rudy D'Angelo, Connecticut
Jeffrey B. Floyd, Virginia
Col. Stuart S. Corning, Jr., Massachusetts
John J. Edwards, Massachusetts
Frank Grant, Canada
Ray Zyla, Mohawk Arms
Bob Learmoth, Massachusetts

Tom Koenig, Ohio
Jack Moore, Ohio
Paul Kaparoff, Ohio
Bill Hammelman, Texas
Ron Wolin, Virginia
George Seymour, Texas
Phillip Weber, Illinois

Foreword

It has been a distinct pleasure and labor of love for Paul Peters and me to gather the medals and decorations assembled on these pages. Thanks to the efforts of many collectors and dealers who also embrace a love of history and appreciation for the beautiful, achieving our goal has been made easier. Between us, Paul and I have spent nearly one hundred years in collecting and dealing in medals and decorations of the world, an experience that has culminated in this opportunity to share our collections with others of like interest. Displayed here are medals and decorations of the United States and Europe up to, but not including, World War II. Within these limits, it was, of course, impossible to include every piece in every category. We have made a concerted effort, however, to present a wide range of those that are most representative in their category. Above all, here are not only the medals collectors can hope to eventually uncover, but also prime examples of the ultimate to strive for in any serious collection.

If only these medals could talk! There would be tales of heroism that stretch from the siege of the Alcazar, to the battle for Belgrad, from the lifting of the Seige of Peking, to the massacre at Adowa and much, much more. The very word "uniform" denotes uniformity and lack of distinguishing features, while only the awards for bravery and meritorious service draw attention to those who have served above and beyond the call of duty. They represent each country's individuality in recognizing the achievements of those who are compelled, for whatever reason, to rise above concerns for their own safety and well-being in order to do that which must be done at all cost. Most such medals are prime examples of the jeweler's art, often utilizing precious metals, fine enamels, and even jewels to create these masterpieces.

However, having won such honors carries with it no assurance that the recipient will be kept from harm's way in the future. On a personal note, when I was recalled to active duty during Korea, I was initially sent with 300 other reservists to Fort Devons, Massachusetts; there, in an effort to eliminate those men who, for one reason or another, should not considered for duty in Korea, i.e., age, physical condition due to wounds, etc. — a special formation was called, at which time, all men who fell into each such category were asked to step forward. Among them was a 66 year old Master Sergeant, whose first Army pay consisted of a silver dollar and two ten dollar gold pieces, who stepped forward for every one of them. In his illustrious career, he had won a DSC, three Silver Stars, and four Purple Hearts (probably from the Indian Wars!), and had already served overseas longer than General Eisenhower. Nevertheless, due to a critical MOS, within three weeks, this grizzled veteran was in Korea with the rest of us.

Values shown reflect the norm which we find at auction, medal society shows, individual sales between dealers and collectors, and as shown in various price guides. It should be understood that numbered and/or named medals will command a premium that will not be reflected in the figures shown.

ALBANIA

The medals and orders of this small, mountainous and backwards country on the Adriatic sea, are, on the whole, most colorful, though few in number. The orders did not proliferate until after the first World War, and, it appears that King Zog was not above selling them to raise cash for the Royal Treasury! Many of these military awards were manufactured in Italy and Austria, and show the pride of workmanship of those countries' artisans.

Star of the Grand Cross of the Order of Skanderbeg. Ray Zyla, Mohawk Arms.

Accession Medal of Prince William of Wied, 3/17/1914.

Reverse of the Accession Medal of Prince William of Wied.

AUSTRIA

The history of Austria, one of the first to present orders and decorations for military valor, is well illustrated in the pieces they produced and awarded over the centuries. Austrian jewelers were especially renowned for their mastery of the medal makers' art, so much so in fact, that over the years many other countries have depended on their expertise for the production of their own medals and decorations.

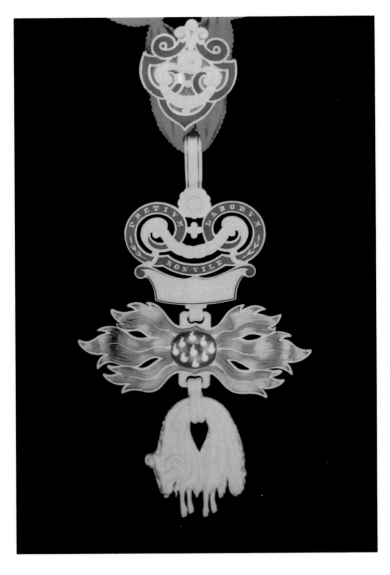

Neck Badge of the Order of the Golden Fleece.

First Class Star, Order of the Iron Crown.

First Class Badge of the Order of the Iron Crown.

Second Class Badge of the Order of the Iron Crown.

Star of the Grand Cross, Order of Leopold (1808-1817).

Commander's Cross, Order of Leopold (1820).

First Class Badge of the Franz Joseph Order, with Crown and Swords.

Maria - Theresien Order (1757-1918).

The Second Class Cross of Merit, the one on the right with
War Decoration (Laurel wreath).

From left to right: The Military Medal of Merit in Silver
with Swords; The Military Medal of Merit in Silver with 2
clasps, representing repeated awards; The Military Medal
of Merit in Gilt, with Swords.

Order of the Tirolian Nobility — while not military in nature, it could be worn while in uniform.

The Jubilee Commemorative Medal for Military personnel.

From left to right, The Karl Wound Medal for 2 wounds; the Karl Wound Medal for 4 wounds.

1908 Jubilee Medal.

The Jubilee Cross for Military personnel.

The Jubilee Medal.

The Sea Voyage medal of 1892-1893; came in both silver and bronze.

Gold Cross of Merit with Crown.

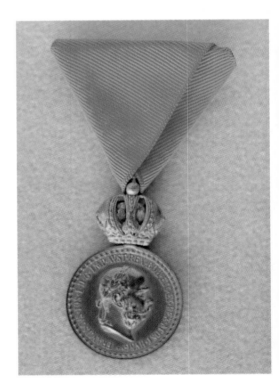

Iron Cross of Merit.

The Karl "Truppenkreuz," or the Karl Cross, for all
Austrian troops who served in World War I.

Gilt Military Medal of Merit.

Large Silver Bravery Medal, First Class.

The small Bronze Bravery Medal on the left, with the small Silver Bravery Medal on the right.

From left to right, the "Signum Memoriae" medal; the 1873
War Medal,; The Franz Joseph Commemoration Medal; the
"Signum Laudus" Medal.

A group of Long Service Medals, from left to right: The
Third Class Military Service Medal for 25 years; the NCO
Long Service Cross for 12 years; the NCO Long Service
Cross for 6 years; the NCO Long Service Cross for 5 years.

The Commemoration Cross in connection with the Balkan Crisis of 1912-1913.

Silver Medal of honor of the Red Cross. John Edwards

Gilt Medal of Honor of the Red Cross.

From left to right: the Tyrol Medal; the Commemorative
Medal for World War I service.

From left to right: The Imperial Pilot's Badge; The Imperial
Observer Badge.

First Class Badge of the Military Order of Merit.

First Class Star of the Honor Badge for Merit.

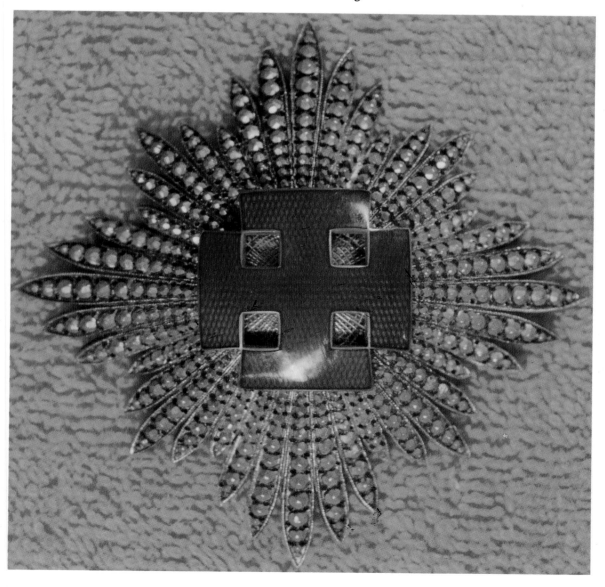

BELGIUM

The orders and decorations of Belgium well reflect the history of the country and its rulers. While attractive, the medals themselves are not rare, since most awards were made by document, with the recipient going directly to the manufacturer, or jeweler to order the award for which he was qualified. It was also possible for anyone who so desired to also avail themselves of this service and order whatever medals appealed to their ego — and pocketbook.

Star of the Grand Cross of the Order of Leopold.

Grand Cross of the Order of Leopold.

Officer, Military, of the Order of Leopold.

Star of the Grand Cross, Maritime, of the Order of Leopold.

Officer, Maritime, of the Order of Leopold.

Star of the Grand Officer, Military, of the Order of Leopold.

Star of the Grand Officer, Maritime, of the Order of Leopold.

Star of the Grand Cross of the Order of the Crown.

Star of the Grand Officer of the Order of the Crown.

Palms to the Order of the Crown.

Medal of the Order of the Crown.

Officer's Cross of the Order of the Crown.

Commander of the Grand Cross of the Order of the Crown.

Grand Cross of the Order of Leopold II.

Knight's cross of the Order of Leopold II.

Star of the Grand Cross of the Order of Leopold II.

Medal of the Order of Leopold II.

First Class Military
Decoration for Merit.

First Class Military Cross.

Second Class Military
Cross.

Second Class Military
Decoration for Merit.

Officer of the Order of the
Lion.

Officer of the Order of the
Star of Africa.

Military Decoration Long
Service Medal, Albert I.
Jeff Floyd

1870-1871 Commemora-
tion Medal. Jeff Floyd

Croix de Guerre

BULGARIA

The influences exerted by Russia, Germany and France over the years can be seen in the orders and decorations of Bulgaria, with many of the medals having been made in Russia during the early days of the Bulgarian monarchy. Bulgarian orders for bravery closely follow the model of the Imperial Russian orders. Austrian influence is also apparent in the use of trifold ribbons, and, eventually, many of the awards were, in fact, made by Austrian jewelers. The artisanship of the enameled orders is especially attractive.

Star of the National Order of Military Merit.

First Class Cross of the National Order of Military Merit.

From left to right: Knight's Cross of the National Order of Military Merit with War decoration; Cross of the National Order of Military Merit with Crown suspension.

Cross of the National Order of Military Merit.

Reverse of the Commander's Cross of the Order of Saint Alexander.

Commander's Cross of the Order of Saint Alexander, with swords on the ring. Established by Prince Alexander in 1879 honoring Saint Alexander Nevsky.

From the left to right: The Silver Soldier's Cross for Bravery; the War Medal, 1915-1918, awarded in 1933; The Bronze Soldier's Medal for Bravery.

Medal of Merit, Boris III. Jeff Floyd

The Order of Merit Medal, Ferdinand.

From left to right, the Order of Merit, Ferdinand and the
Order of merit with Crown, Ferdinand

Bulgarian Red Cross Medal.   Reverse Bulgarian Red Cross Medal.

Bulgarian 1908 Commemorative Medal.

Bulgaria Military Merit Medal 1878 with swords.

CZECHOSLOVAKIA

Since it did not become a state until after the defeat of the Central Powers in World War I, the medals and orders of Czechoslovakia reflect the age old influences of Bohemia, Moravia and Slovakia, with many heroes of antiquity, becoming part of the heritage of modern Czechoslovakia. While only limited medals were produced, all clearly show the artistic background of its countrymen.

The War Service Medal, 1914-1918; note the brass soldier's badge attached to the ribbon.

Commander's Order of the Lion of Czechoslovakia.

The Bohemia Cross, 1814.

Medal for Service to the Homeland. Jeff Floyd

Cross for Faithful Service, 1938. Jeff Floyd

Commemorative Cross for Volunteers, 1918-1919; awarded
to those in action in Slovakia against the Hungarian
Communist troops of Bela Kun.

Medal for Conscription. Jeff Floyd

Medal bar for service with the Czech Legion in France during World War I; from left to right: The Czechoslovakian War Cross; Czechoslovakian Legion Medal; The Czechoslovakian Victory Medal; French Croix de Guerre; French World war I Commemorative Medal, 1914-1918. Frank Grant

DENMARK

With the exception of the Order of the Dannebrog, which is encountered, though infrequently, most Danish orders must be returned to the Crown upon the death of the recipient. While attractive and interesting in their historical context, Denmark's orders, decorations and medals are not at the top of a collector's list of acquisitions.

Top: Collar of the Order of the Dannebrog.
Top center: Badge of the Grand Commander of the Order of the Dannebrog.
Bottom left: Star of the Grand Cross, with diamonds, of the Order of the Dannebrog.
Bottom right: Star of the Grand Commander and the Grand Cross of the Order of the Dannebrog.
Bottom center: Badge of the Grand Cross of the Order of the Dannebrog.
Top left: Cross of the Commander, 1st Degree, and the Commander, of the Order of the Dannebrog.

Top right: Breast Cross, Commander 1st Degree of the Order of the Dannebrog.
Bottom left: Kinght's Cross, 1st degree of the Order of the Dannebrog.
Bottom right: Knight's Cross of the Order of the Dannebrog.
Bottom center: Silver Cross of the Order of the Dannebrog.

The Royal Medal of Recompense. Jeff Floyd

Another view of the Cross, Commander 1st Degree of the
Order of the Dannebrog

Another view of the Knight's Cross of the Order of the
Dannebrog.

FINLAND

Finland, a country long subjugated by Russia, reflects this Russian influence in its awards, especially those for bravery. With their fine enameling and metal work, Finland's orders are especially attractive, showing a traditional yet innovative approach to design. Insofar as their independence is concerned, this country's relatively short history carries with it a legacy of bravery and devotion to liberty exceeded by none.

Star of the Grand Cross of the Cross of Liberty, with Swords.

First Class Cross of the Cross of Liberty.

Third Class Cross of the Cross of Liberty.

First Class Mannerheim Cross of the Cross of Liberty.

Second Class Badge of the Mannerheim Cross of the Cross of Liberty, Pin Back.

Left: Second Class Medal of Liberty.

Center: Medal of Merit, Cross of Liberty.

Right: First Class Medal of Liberty.

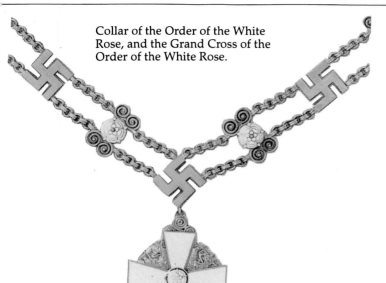

Collar of the Order of the White Rose, and the Grand Cross of the Order of the White Rose.

Left: Knight's Cross of the Order of the White Rose.
Right: Medal of the Order of the White Rose.

First Class Commander of the Order of the White Rose.

Star of the First Class Commander of the Order of the White Rose.

Star of the Commander of the Grand Cross of the Order of the White Rose.

Star of the Commander of the Grand Cross of the Order of the Lion.

First Class Commander of the Order of the Lion.

Cross of Merit of the Order of the Lion.

Commander of the Grand Cross of the Order of the Lion.

War of Liberty Medal, 1918. Jeff Floyd

FRANCE

Due in large part to the tumultuous history of France during the last three hundred years, the collector is presented with a vast panoply of medals, decorations and orders celebrating Kingdoms, Empires, and Republics. There are enormous variations in the quality of the styles and manufacture of many of these French awards, ranging from the exquisite to the poorly-cast products more recently seen on the market. The variety of French medals offers the collector unusual opportunities, from exploring the area of Colonial decorations, which is a wholly separate field, to viewing the period-to-period progression that appears throughout the history of the same medal. Overall, France has produced some of the most beautiful awards available to the public.

Star of the Grand Cross of the Legion of Honor, 1811, type 2.

Grand Cross of the Legion of Honor 1814, the Bourbon Restoration, type 3.

Star of the Grand Cross of the Legion of Honor'- 3rd
Republic.

Grand Cross of the Legion of Honor - Republic, 1870-1951.

Knight of the Legion of Honor.

Star of the Grand Cross of the Legion of Honor, 1864.

Grand Cross of the Legion of Honor, 1864.

The Military Medal, established by Napoleon III in 1852;
France's second highest military decoration.

The St. Helena Medal.

Croix de Guerre with palm, World War I.

The Verdun Medal, given by the city of Verdun to World War I Allies who served there.

Wound Medal, World War I.

The Dardanelles Medal.

The St. Mihiel Medal, given to World War I Allied troops by the city of St. Mihiel.

World War I Veteran's Society Medal.

The Italian Campaign Medal, 1859.

The Campaign in Mexico, 1862-1865

Franco-Prussian War 1870 Red Cross Medal.

The Tonkin Medal, for campaigns in Indo-China, 1883-1893.

Officer's Cross of the Order of the Black Star.

The War Cross, T.O.E., i.e., the Foreign Theatre of Operations.

Officer's Cross of the Order of the Anjouan Star.

Officer of the Order of Nichan-el-Anouar.

GERMANY - STATES

Due to the overwhelming quantity and diversity of overlapping orders, awards, decorations and medals given by the different German states, it is practically impossible to collect and show for consideration the myriad of pieces that have emerged over the years.

The field of German medals is particularly large and complex, capable of filling a volume of its own, however on the following pages is an extensive sampling of many outstanding and readily identifiable decorations and medals. The following presentation has been arranged by order of importance of the states themselves, as promulgated by the authorities of the time. The states are shown as follows:

PRUSSIA, BAVARIA, SAXONY, WURTTEMBURG, BADEN, HESSE, MECKLENBURG - SCHWERIN, SAXE - WEIMAR, MECKLENBURG - STRELITZ, OLDENBURG, BRAUNSCHWEIG, SAXE - ALTENBURG, SAXE - COBURG - GOTHA, SAXE - MEININGEN, ANHALT, SCHWARZBURG RUDOLSTADT & SONDERHAUSEN, WALDECK, REUSS, SCHAUMBURG - LIPPE, LIPPE, HANSEATIC CITY STATES

Collar, Prussian Order of the Black Eagle.

Star of the Prussian Order of the Black Eagle.

Another view of the Star of the Prussian Order of the Black Eagle, Prussia's highest order.

A variant of the Star of the Prussian Order of the Black Eagle.

A cloth sewn-on variant of the Star of the Prussian Order of the Black Eagle for a cape or mantel.

Another view of the Cross and sash of the Prussian Order of the Black Eagle.

Cross of the Prussian Order of the Black Eagle.

Another close-up view of the Cross of the Prussian Order of the Black Eagle; note the initial 'F' on the obverse of the medal, for King Frederick of Prussia, founder of the Order. This is Prussia's highest decoration, in one class only.

Reverse of the Cross of the Prussian Order of the Black Eagle.

Prussian Order 'Pour Le Merite' or more commonly known as 'The Blue Max'; the First Class Badge of the Grand Cross was awarded only 5 times.

Prussian Order 'Pour Le Merite' with Oak leaf cluster, signifying outstanding bravery. This was the equivalent of the Medal of Honor, or the Victoria Cross.

Prussian Order 'Pour Le Merite', Knight's Cross with Crown for holder for 50 years; oak leaves were awarded for winning the medal a second time.

Star of the Grand Cross of the Prussian Order 'Pour Le Merite.'

Prussian Military Merit Cross in gold awarded to enlisted men for bravery; officers received the 'Pour Le Merite.'

The General Honor Cross.

Collar of the Prussian Order of the Red Eagle.

Star of the Grand Cross of the Prussian Order of the Red Eagle.

Reverse of the Star of the Grand Cross of the Prussian Order of the Red Eagle.

Grand Cross of the Prussian Order of the Red Eagle.

Another view of the Grand Cross of the Prussian Order of the Red Eagle with oak leaves and swords. Came in 6 classes, and was originally founded by Prince William of Brandenburg-Bayreuth as the Order of Sincerity.

Reverse of the Grand Cross of the Prussian Order of the Red Eagle.

First Class Star of the Order of the Red Eagle.

Another view of First Class Badge of the Prussian Order of the Red eagle.

First Class Badge of the Prussian Order of the Red Eagle with Oak Leaves, as worn from the sash.

Reverse of the First Class Badge of the Prussian Order of the Red Eagle.

Star of the First Class Badge of the Prussian Order of the Red Eagle

Second Class Star of the Prussian Order of the Red eagle.

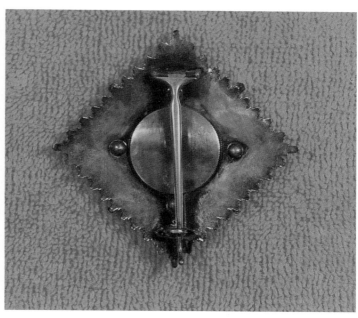

Reverse of the Second Class Star of the Prussian Order of the Red Eagle.

Another view of the Second Class Star to the Prussian Order of the Red Eagle.

Second Class Cross of the Prussian Order of the Red eagle.

Second Class Cross (Neck Badge), with Oak
Leaves of the Prussian Order of the Red Eagle.

Obverse of the Second Class Cross with Oak Leaves of the
Prussian Order of the Red Eagle on war ribbon.

Reverse of the Second Class Cross, on war ribbon, of the
Prussian Order of the Red Eagle.

Fourth Class Cross of the Prussian Order of the Red Eagle.

Third Class Cross of the Prussian Order of the Red Eagle.

Medal of the Order of the Red Eagle.

Fourth Class Cross of the Prussian Order of the Red Eagle, 3rd model.

First Class Star of the Prussian Order of the Crown.

Second Class Star of the Prussian Order of the Crown.

First Class Badge (left) and Third Class Knight's Badge (right) of the Prussian Order of the Crown.

Second Class Cross on war ribbon of the Prussian Order of the Crown.

Fourth Class Cross of the Prussian Order of the Crown.

Medal of the Prussian Order of the Crown.

Grand Cross of the Prussian Order of the Crown.

Star of the Merit Order of the Prussian Crown.

Badge and sash of the Merit Order of the Prussian Crown. This award came in one class only, and from 1901 to 1913, had been awarded only 49 times. Very rare.

Grand Commander's Collar and Badge of the House Order of the Hohenzollern. This award came in 5 classes, and is still being awarded by the Princely House of Hohenzollern on its own authority.

The Commander's Star of the House Order of the Hohenzollern with Swords

Eagle neckpiece of the Order of the House of Hohenzollern.

Reverse of the Eagle neckpiece of the Order of the House of Hohenzollern.

Star of the Grand Commander of the House Order of Hohenzollern.

Eagle Badge of the House Order of the Hohenzollern.

A view of two Knight's
Crosses, with and without
Swords of the Order of the
House of Hohenzollern

The reverse of the two
Knight's Crosses of the
House Order of the
Hohenzollern.

Commander's Cross of the
House Order of the
Hohenzollern.

Knight's Cross with
Swords of the Order of the
House of Hohenzollern.

Reverse of the
Commander's Cross of the
House Order of the
Hohenzollern.

First Class Badge of the Princely House Order of the Hohenzollern.

Second Class Cross of the Princely House Order of the Hohenzollern.

Star of the Order of the Phoenix.

Commander's Cross of the Order of the Phoenix.

Order of the Iron Cross, 1914, the Hindenburg Star. Paul von Hindenburg was the only recipient.

First Class Iron Cross, 1914.

Grand Cross of the Iron Cross, 1914. Awarded only 5 times during World War One.

A view of two Second Class Iron Crosses, 1914; one on the ribbon for non-combatants (left) and the other (right) on the combatants ribbon. The former is much less frequently encountered.

The Second Class Iron Cross, 1870-1871, with Oak Leaves, '25', and on a non-combattant's ribbon.

Two Prussian Red Cross medals, the one on the left, the Second Class medal in silver with enamel cross, while the one on the right is the Third class medal in bronze.

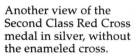

Cross of Merit for War Aid, World War I.

Another view of the Second Class Red Cross medal in silver, without the enameled cross.

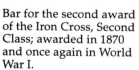

Bar for the second award of the Iron Cross, Second Class; awarded in 1870 and once again in World War I.

War Service medal, second model with "WR" monogram.

1864 War Service medal on combattant's ribbon.

Duppel Storm Cross, for the Danish War of 1864.

The 1866 War against Austria, to the left, the 'Main Army' cross and to the right, the Loyal Fighter Cross.

Campaign medal for the Franco-Prussian War, with bar "SEDAN."

Franco-Prussian War four medal bar, from left to right: the Iron Cross Second Class, with a rarely seen device; the Red Cross Medal; the 1870-1871 War Medal with four bars; lastly, the Centenary Medal.

South West Africa Service Medal, 1904-1905, for the Herrero Rebellion; on the left, the steel medal for non-combattant with bar "Herreroland", and on the right the gilt medal for combatants.

Boxer Rebellion (China) Service Medal, gilt for combatants and steel for non-combatants.

The Centenary Medal.

The Hamburg Cross, issued Post-War to war veterans of Hamburg.

The three classes of badges awarded by the German Army for wounds during World War One; the Black Badge for a single wound, the Silver Badge for three or more wounds, and the Gold Badge for grievous wounds.

The three classes of badges awarded by the German Navy for wounds received during World War One; the Black Badge for one or more wounds, the Silver Badge for three or more wounds, and the gold Badge for grievous wounds.

The three variations of the Cross of Honor, awarded well after World War One, as follows: From the left, for non-comb atants, the middle, for combatants (with swords), and on the right, for the next-of-kin for the fallen.

Three medal Medal Bar, with three World War One veteran's medals; from the left, the Naval Flanders Cross, with bar "FLANDERNSCHLAGHT" and bar "SERBIEN," Veteran League Medal with swords, and last an Austrian Veteran's medal, with swords.

The Colonial Medal, known as the "Elephant Order."

War Veteran's medal on an unusual ribbon mount.

The Second Class Silesian Eagle.

Left: Unauthorized Verdun Veteran's Medal.
Center: Veteran's Association Medal.
Right: Somme Veteran's Medal, unauthorized.

20 year Long Service Cross.

Faithful Service Medal, silver; 9 years, gilt; 12 years.

2nd Class Faithful Service Medal, Reserves.

25 year Long Service Cross.

Faithful Service Medal, Silver; 9 years, Gilt; 12 years.

Other Ranks Faithful Service in the Reserves Medal.

Black Wound badge as awarded to members of the "Condor Legion" for wounds received during the Spanish Civil War, 1936-1939.

Collar of the Order of Saint Hubert.

Grand Cross of the Order of Saint Hubert.

The Knight's Star of the Order of Saint Hubert.

Collar of the House Order of Saint George.

Star of the Order of Saint George, in its presentation case.

Commander's Cross of the House Order of Saint George.

Star for the Grand Cross for the Order of St. Michael.

Collar of the Order of St. Michael.

Grand Cross of the Order of St. Michael.

Commander's Cross of the Order of St. Michael. This is a neck badge.

Reverse of the Knight's Cross of the Order of St. Michael.

Merit Medal of the Order of St. Michael.

Merit Cross of St. Michael.

Collar of the Military Order of Maximilian - Joseph.

Star of the Military Order of Maximilian - Joseph (1814).

Grand Cross of the Military Order of
Maximilian - Joseph.

Another view of the Grand Cross of the
Military Order of Maximilian - Joseph.

Knight's Cross with
Crown of the Military
Order of Maximilian -
Joseph.

Star of the Grand Cross of
the Order of Military
Merit.

Grand Cross of the Order
of Military Merit.

Second Class Cross with
Swords of the Order of
Military Merit.

Merit Cross with Swords
of the Order of Military
Merit

Officer's Cross of the Order of Military Merit, pin back.

Medal Bar, World War I, from left to right: The Iron Cross, second class; The medal for Military Merit, with Swords; The Sanitats Orden — extremely rare, with approximately 200 being awarded. Note the miniatures of the medals on the watch fob.

Third Class Cross to the Order of Military Merit, on the left; on the right, the Second Class Cross of the Order of Military Merit. These were awarded to enlisted men.

Fourth Class (Silver) Cross with Swords of the Order of Military Merit, with war ribbon.

The Order of Ludwig.

The Silver Medal for
Bravery, Maximilian-
Joseph.

Reverse of the Silver
Medal for Bravery.

Life Saving Medal.

The Cross of King Ludwig.

1866 Austrian War Cross.

Red Cross Medal, World War I. Stu Corning.

Bavarian 24 year Service Medal.

1905 Army Jubilee Medal.

Bavarian 9 year Faithful Service Medal.

Bavarian Reserves 2nd Class Service Medal.

Star of the Order of the Crown
of Rue.

Another view of the Star of the Order
of the Crown of Rue.

Star of the Military Order of Saint Henry.

Grand Cross of the Military Order
of Saint Henry.

Grand Cross of the Order of the Crown
of Rue.

Knight's Cross of the Military Order
of Saint Henry.

Medal of the Military Order of Saint Henry.

Star of the Grand Cross of the Order of Merit.

Grand Cross of the Order of Merit.

Star of the Grand Cross of the Order of Albert.

Knight's Cross with Swords of the Order of Merit.

Commander's Star of the Order of Merit.

Grand Cross of the Order of Albert

Commander's Star of the Order of Albert.

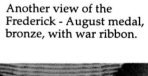

Another view of the
Frederick - August medal,
bronze, with war ribbon.

Commander' Cross with Swords
of the Order of Albert.

Officer's Cross with Swords of the
Order of Albert.

Frederick - August Medal, bronze,
with war ribbon.

War Service Cross.

War Pledge Cross, 1914-1918

War Merit Medal.

War Merit Honor Cross with combattant's ribbon.

Long Service Medals, on the left for nine (9) years, and on the right for twelve (12) years.

Star of the Grand Cross of the Order of the Wurttemburg Crown.

Commander's Cross of the Order of the Wurttemburg Crown.

Grand Cross, with Crown and Swords, of the Order of the Wurttemburg Crown.

Commander's Star of the Order of the Wurttemburg Crown.

Knight's Honor Cross of the Order of the Wurttemburg Crown.

Star with Swords of the
Grand Cross of the Order
of Frederick.

Knight's Cross of the Order of the
Wurttemburg Crown.

Grand Cross with Swords
of the Order of Frederick.

Star of the Commander's
Cross of the Order of
Frederick.

Commander's Cross of the Order of Frederick.

Another view of the
Commander's Cross of the
Order of Frederick.

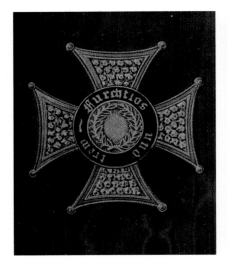

Star of the Grand Cross to the Order of Military Merit.

Grand Cross of the Order of Military Merit.

Knight's cross of the Order of Military Merit.

Merit Cross.

Jubilee Medal.

Merit Medal of the Order of the Crown.

Wilhelm Cross with Swords, World War One, pin back.

Charlotten Medal.

Wilhelm Cross without Swords.

On the left, the Gilt Military Medal, with, on the right, the Silver Military Medal.

Wilhelm Cross without Swords.

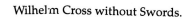

Collar of the Order of Berthold.

Star of the Grand Cross of the Order of Berthold.

Collar of the House Order of Fidelity.

Star of the House Order of Fidelity.

Badge of the House Order of Fidelity.

Grand Cross of the Order of Berthold.

Knight's Cross with
Swords of the Order of
Berthold.

Star of the Grand Cross of
the Order of the Zahringen
Lion.

Grand Cross with Swords
of the Order of the
Zahringen Lion.

Star of the Commander's
Cross of the Order of the
Zahringen Lion.

Commander's Cross with
Swords of the Order of the
Zahringen Lion.

On the right is the First
Class Knight's Cross in
gold of the Order of the
Zahringen Lion, while on
the left is the Second Class
Knight's Cross with
Swords and Oak Leaves in
silver of the Order of the
Zahringen Lion.

Merit Cross of the Zahringen Lion.

Star of the Military Order
of Charles Frederick.

Grand Cross of the
Military Order of Charles
Frederick.

Knight's Cross of the
Military Order of Charles
Frederick.

Silver Service Medal, 1916-1918

Frederick - Louisa Medal.

War Merit Cross.

Volunteer War Help Medal.

1849 War Medal.

Collar of the House Order
of the Golden Lion.

Star of the Grand Cross of
the Order of Ludwig.

Another view of the Badge
of the Order of the Golden
Lion.

Star of the Order of the Golden Lion.

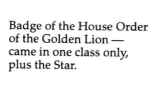

Badge of the House Order
of the Golden Lion —
came in one class only,
plus the Star.

Grand Cross of the Order of Ludwig.

Commander's Star of the
Order of Ludwig.

Commander's Cross (1st
and 2nd) of the Order of
Ludwig.

Commander's Star First
Class of the Order of
Philip.

Grand Cross of the Order of Philip.

Star of the Grand Cross of
the Order of Philip.

Commander's Cross of the Order of Philip.

Honor Cross of the Order
of Philip.

First Class Commander's
Cross of the Order of the
Star of Brabant.

Second Class Grand
Commander's Star of the
Order of The Star of
Brabant

First Class Silver Cross of
the Order of the Star of
Brabant.

Military Merit Cross.

Merit Cross of the Order of
Philip, with Swords.

Life Saving Medal.

The Silver War Service Medal.

War Honor Medal.

War Merit Badge, pin back.

Collar, as awarded to the
Schwerin family, of the
House Order of the
Wendian Crown.

Star of the Grand Cross of
the Order of the Wendian
Crown.

Grand Cross of the Order
of the Wendian Crown.

Star of the Grand Com-
mander of the Order of the
Wendian Crown.

Commander's Cross of the
Order of the Wendian
Crown.

Star of the Grand Cross of
the Order of the Griffin.

Commander's Star of the
Order of the Griffin.

Grand Cross of the Order
of the Griffin.

Honor Cross of the Order
of the Griffin.

Cross for outstanding War
Service, non-combattant.

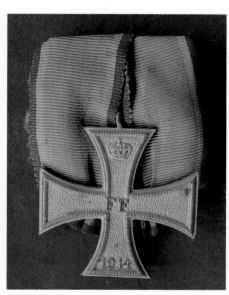

The Second Class Military Merit
Medal.

War Service Medal.

Star of the Grand Cross of
the Order of the White
falcon.

Grand Cross of the Order
of the White Falcon.

Commander's Star of the
Order of the White Falcon.

Commander's Cross of the
Order of the White Falcon.

First Class Knight's Cross
of the Order of the White
Falcon.

Second Class Knight's
Cross of the Order of the
White Falcon.

Merit Cross

Medal of Merit.

Wilhelm-Ernst War Cross.

Honor Cross for War related Service.

Collar of the House and Merit Order of Peter Frederick Louis.

Star of the Grand Cross of the House and Merit Order of Peter Frederick Louis.

Grand Cross of the House and Merit Order of Peter Frederick Louis.

Officer's Cross of the House and Merit Order of Peter Frederick Louis.

Commander's Cross of the House and Merit Order of Peter Frederick Louis.

Knight's Cross of the House and Merit Order of Peter Frederick Louis.

The Honor Cross.

On the left, the Frederick August Cross 2nd Class with combattant ribbon, World War One, and, on the right, the Frist Class Frederick August Cross, Pin Back, World War One.

Grand Cross of the Order of Henry the Lion.

First Class Cross of the Order of Henry the Lion.

First Class Star of the Order of Henry the Lion.

Commander's Star of the Order of Henry the Lion.

Left: Commander's Neck Badge, Order of Henry the Lion.

Right: Reverse of the Commander's Neck Badge, Order of Henry the Lion.

Left: War Service Cross with Combattant's clasp.

Right: Lifesaving Medal.

Collar of the Ernestine House Order.

The Star of the Ernestine House Order.

Grand Cross of the Ernestine House Order.

Commander's Star of the Ernestine House Order.

Silver Service Cross of the Ernestine House Order.

Reverse of the War Service Medal.

Jubilee Medal.

Karl - Edward War Cross, 1916-1918.

Karl - Edward Military Service Medal with 1914-1918 War device.

First Class Knight's Cross, Ernestine House Order, showing the presentation case.

First Class Knight's Cross, Ernestine House Order, within the presentation case.

Collar of the House Order of Albert the Bear.

Commander's Star of the House Order of Albert the Bear.

Friedreich Cross with the ribbon for non-combattant.

Grand Cross of the House
Order of Albert the Bear.

Knight's Cross with
Swords of the Hotse Order
of Albert the Bear.

Second Class
Knight's Cross of
the Honor Cross.

First Class Cross of the Honor Cross.

Third Class Knight's Cross of the Honor Cross.

The Honor Medal.

The Jubilee Medal.

Third Class Cross with Swords of the Order of Merit.

War Service Medal with Swords.

First Class Cross with Crown of the Order of Merit.

Gold Medal For Merit.

Officer's Cross with Swords of the Honor Cross.

First Class Honor Cross.

Fourth Class Honor Cross.

War Service Cross, Pin Back.

The War Service Medal for Women.

First Class Cross with Swords of the Order of the Honor of the House of Lippe.

Second Class Cross of the Order of the Honor of the House of Lippe.

War Cross, 1914-1918, with combattant's ribbon.

Cross for Loyal Service, 1914-1918, with non-combattant's ribbon.

Medal for Merit, World War I.

Medal For Red Cross Military Service.

Star of the Cross of Honor
of the House of Lippe.

Second Class Cross of the
Cross of Honor of the
House of Lippe.

Second Class Cross of the
Order of Leopold, fourth
type with swallow.

Gold Medal of Merit, second type.

War Merit Cross, 1914-1918.

War Honor Medal for combattant.

On the left, the Hanseatic Cross, Lubeck; in the middle, the
Hanseatic Cross, Hamburg, and on the right, the Hanseatic
Cross, Bremen.

Life Saving Medal of the City of Bremen.

GREAT BRITAIN

Invariably made to the highest standard of design and quality, the awards of Great Britain comprise form one of the most beautiful areas of collecting, as well as one of the most challenging. There is meticulous control over the numbers of various orders and decorations produced, and additionally, in many instances the earning of a higher award obligated the honoree to return the lower orders to the Crown. The collector will find a world of history in these medals and decorations of the British Empire — over which, at the time, "The sun never sets."

Second Class Order of the Bath.

Collar of the most Noble Order of the Garter and, Badge of the most Noble Order of the Garter.

Star of the Most Noble Order of the Garter.

Military Medal of the Order of Merit.

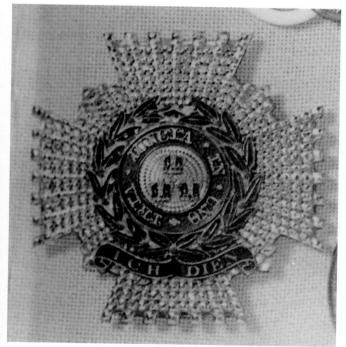

Star of the Military Knight Commander of the Order of the Bath.

Military Knight Commander of the Order of the Bath.

Left: Star of the Knight Commander of the Order of the British Empire.
Center: Knight's Grand Cross of the Order of the British Empire.
Right: Cross of the Knight Commander and Commander of the Order of the British Empire.

Star of the Knight's Grand Cross of the Order of the British Empire.

Officer's Medal of the Order of the British Empire.

The Victoria Cross.

The Distinguished Service Order.

The George Cross.

The Distinguished Service Cross.

The Distinguished Flying Cross.

The Military Cross.

GREECE

In 1821, Greece revolted against the centuries of domination by the Turkish Empire, attaining her independence in 1822. This struggle, as well as the religious influences of Greek life are reflected in the beautiful awards of this country. Obliged to go to war against Turkey several additional times in the last 171 years, Greece was also reluctantly involved in World War I. Over the years, England appears to have been responsible for the manufacture of the majority of Greek awards, and this quality of British workmanship is apparent in many of the beautiful pieces shown here.

Star of the Grand Cross and the Grand Commander of the Order of the Phoenix.

Left: Fourth Class Cross of the Order of the Phoenix.
Right: Fifth Class Cross ot the Order of the Phoenix.

Grand Cross of the Order of the Phoenix.

Above:
Bottom center: Star of the Grand Cross of the Order of the Saviour.
Top: Grand Cross of the Order of the Saviour.
Bottom left: Fourth Class Cross of the Order of the Saviour.
Bottom right: Fifth Class Cross of the Order of the Saviour.

Far Left: The Bronze order of George I. Jeff Floyd

Left: Turkish War Medal, 1912-1913, for combatant. Jeff Floyd

HUNGARY

Until 1918, the awards of Hungary were closely associated with Austria; some awards were considered a continuation, such as the Order of Saint Stephan. Other awards were established or revived after the birth of the Regency of Admiral Horthy; which occurred in 1920 after the defeat of the Communist forces of Bela Kun. The style as well as the system of awards closely follows the Austrian, as found in the use of tri-fold ribbons, rosettes and various ribbon devices.

Grand Cross of the Order of Saint Stephan (1810).

Star of the Grand Cross of the Order of Saint Stephan.

Commemorative Medal for Participation in World War I.

World War I Commemorative Medal

The Upper Hungary Medal. Jeff Floyd

Left: Knight's Cross of the Order of Merit.

Right: Fire Cross for combatants. Jeff Floyd

Left: Second Class Officer's 25 Year Long Service Cross. Jeff Floyd

Right: Bronze "Signum Laudis" Medal with Swords. Jeff Floyd

Large Silver Bravery
Medal (Horthx). Jeff Floyd

Small Silver Bravery
Medal (Horthy). Jeff floyd

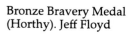

Bronze Bravery Medal
(Horthy). Jeff Floyd

ITALY

A h, Italy, Bella Italia, with its myriad of flamboyantly beautiful decorations and orders, classicist medals of the jeweler's art. In reviewing the history of Italian awards, they are striking in their similarity to the independent states of Germany prior to unification. Italy was then a group of independent states, and were unified under the stronger Piedmont-Sardinia, with each state having formulated its own orders. Upon unification in 1875, the awards of Piedmont-Sardinia became the awards of the Kingdom of Italy. These replaced the awards previously made by the other states.

Well designed and manufactured, Italian medals can prove to have a rightful place in anyone's general collection. As an example, look at the quality of the colonial medals, with the figures appearing to come right off the face of the medal! Commemorative medals also play a big part in the Italian love affair with medals, with individual units awarding their own medals for the war as well as for individual battles.

First Class Star of the Military Order of Saint Savoy.

First Class Cross of the Military Order of Saint Savoy.

Cross of the Order of the Crown, founded in 1868 by King Emmanuel; comes in 5 classes.

Knight's Cross of the Order of the Crown. Rudy D'Angelo

Miniature Medal of the Order of the Crown. Rudy D'Angelo

Cross of the Grand Officer and Commander of the Military Order of Italy.

Officer's Cross of the Military Order of Italy.

Star of the Grand Cross of the Military Order of Italy.

World War I commemorative silver medal awarded to the 37th Infantry Division, which did not retreat, and whose motto was, "We will not surrender as long as one man still stands." The division fought 1915/1916 in numerous battles against the Austrians. Rudy D'Angelo

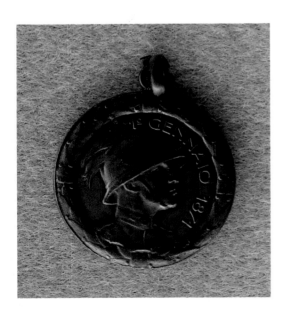

Medal for service in the 9th Bersaglieri Brigade, 1871, one year after they took over Rome's Porta Pia, thus making unification complete. Rudy D'Angelo

Bronze medal for the coronation of King Victor Emmanuel III, 29 July 1900. Rudy D' Angelo

World War I commemorative medal for service with the "Guastatori" demolition and assault troops. On the left, the 81st Infantry Assault Regiment, while on the right, the 9th Alpine Demolition Company. 1915-1918. Rudy D'Angelo

Silver medal honoring the Duke of Aosta, who led the Italian 3rd Atmy Corps in World War I. It was issued as a memorial upon his death in 1934. Rudy D'Angelo

On the left, the Cross for Military Valor; on the right, the Cross for War Merit. Rudy D'Angelo

On the left, the Bronze Medal for Military Valor, issued from 1887; on the right, the Silver Medal for Military Valor, issued from 1833. Royal Italian Army, for highest honor. Rudy D'Angelo

Bronze medal for Italian unity after World War I, commemoration the Wars of Independence from 1848-1918, showing a bust of King Victor Emmanuel. Rudy D'Angelo

The Silver Medal for Italian Independence and Unity under King Victor Emmanuel II, first king of united Italy. Authorized in 1862. Rudy D'Angelo

The Silver Medal for Italian Independence and Unity, 1848-1870. Authorized by King Umberto I in 1883. Rudy D'Angelo

The Bronze Medal for African Campaigns 1887-1897, under King Umberto I; created in 1894 for all African colonial campaigns. Rudy D'Angelo

World War I Service Medal, made from the bronze of captured Austrian cannons. This medal has bars 1915-1918, as well as the rare bar for Albania, 1920. Rudy D'Angelo

The Silver Medal for service in the Italo-Turkish War, 1911-1912; this was also known as the Libyan Service Medal. Rudy D'Angelo

Rare World War I Bronze Medal awarded to the Czechoslovakian troops serving on the Italian front under Italian command. Rudy D'Angelo

Silver and white enamel Cross for World War I service in the 3rd Army, commanded by the Duke of Aosta. This was awarded right at the end of the War, becoming the first commemorative cross for World War I service. Rudy D'Angelo

Silver Medal for Loyal Command in the Royal Italian Army, World War I. Rudy D'Angelo

Silver World War I Bersaglieri Medal for Service in the 5th Bersaglieri Brigade, awarded July, 1918. Rudy D'Angelo

Extremely rare Service Cross in Gold and enamel for the Italian Expeditionary Corps serving in the Balkans, principally Albania and Macedonia in World War I. Rudy D'Angelo

Silver Medal in Honor of Italian Royal Infantrymen in World War I; awarded in 1920. Rudy D'Angelo

World War I Cross for service in the Assault Corps, Arditi of Italy; awarded in the early 1920s. Rudy D'Angelo

Bronze Medal for the Mothers of the Fallen, World War I. Rudy D'Angelo

Silver Commemorative Medal awarded to families of the Royal Carabinieri form Bari killed in action in World War I. Rudy D'Angelo

Bronze Medal for the occupation and liberation of Fiume, 12 September 1919. Rudy D'Angelo

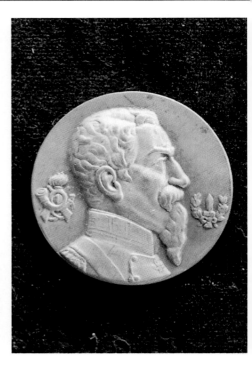

Bronze Medallion honoring General Lamarmora who organized the Royal Bersaglieri Corps in 1836. he died in the Crimean War in 1855. Rudy D'Angelo

Silver Medal for service in the elite Bersaglieri Corps (sharpshooters) in World War I. Rudy D'Angelo

World War I Silver Medal for service with the 35th Artillery Regiment of the "Acqui" division. Rudy D'Angelo

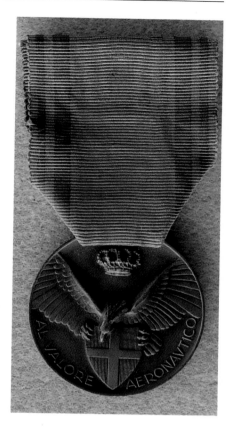

Royal Italian Navy Bronze Medal of Honor for Long Command, awarded for 10, 15 and 20 years of Naval Navigation Command. Rudy D'Angelo

The Cross for 26 years in Military Service, also called the Army Seniority Cross, shown with and without the Royal Savoy Crown suspension. Awarded during the reign of King Victor Emmanuel III. Rudy D'Angelo

Bronze Medal for Aeronautical Valor in the Royal Italian Air Force; instituted 1927. Rudy D'Angelo

Silver Medal awarded to Italian Legionnaires and colored troops who took part in the Italo-Ethiopian War, 3 October 1935 to 9 May 1936. Fascist issue. Rudy D'Angelo

Official Bronze Medal with bar "FERT" for the Italo-Ethiopian War, 1935-1936. Rudy D'Angelo

On the left, the official Medal for Fascist Campaigns, 1919-1922. On the right is the Fascist issued Medal for the March on Rome, 28 October 1922. Rudy D'Angelo

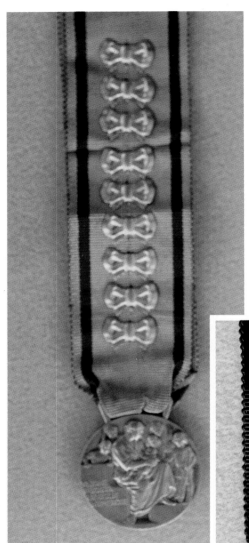

An interesting, non-military medal is the Fascist Mother's Medal awarded to prolific mothers ! Each bow represented another child for the fascist Regime, in this case, nine ! Rudy D'Angelo

The Bronze Cross for ten years in the MVSN, the Fascist Militia for National Security. Rudy D'Angelo

Extemely rare Silver and Black enamel medal worn by the "Moschettieri del Duce," the bodyguards of Mussolini. Rudy D'Angelo

The Gold Medal for the Royal Infantry Tactics School. Rudy D'Angelo

Italian Colonial Troops Service Medals — RCTC — the Royal Corps of Colonial Troops. From the left: the 45th Muslim Battalion, for service in Ethiopia; the 16th Colonial Battalion of Eritrean Troops; The Eritrean Army Corps under Italian Command during the Ethiopian War; The Medal for service in the Libyan Camel Corps under Italian Command (Meharisti). Rudy D'Angelo

The Spanish Order of Military Merit Medal as awarded to Italians who participated in the Spanish Civil War, 1936-1939. Rudy D'Angelo

A grouping of miniature medals, from left to right: 10 years service in the Fascist Militia; Cross for World War I service in Assault Troops (Arditi); Order of St. Maurizio and St. Lazzaro; World War I Service Medal, 1915-1918. Rudy D'Angelo

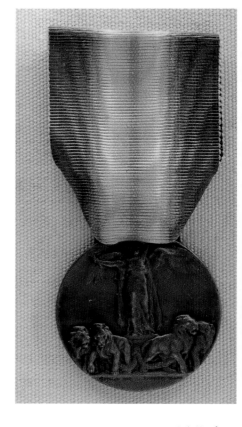

World War One Victory Medal. Rudy D'Angelo

Grouping of World War I miniature medals, from left to right: Italian Unity, 1848-1918; The Allied Victory Medal; The War Merit Cross; The War Service Medal, 1915-1918. Rudy D'Angelo

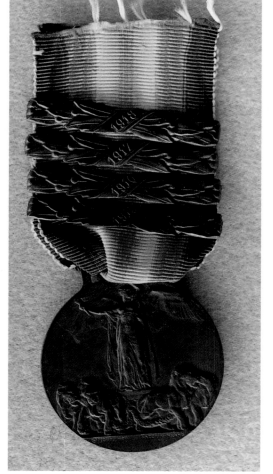

Italian World War I Victory Medal, with bars 1915-1918. Rudy D'Angelo

Medals awarded to the Italians for the Spanish Civil War, 1936-1939: Medal for the War for Liberation and Unity of Spain, 1936-1939; Spanish issue medal for Italians and Germans; Spanish issue, a variation of the preceding, 17 July 1936; Cross of the Spanish Campaign. Rudy D'Angelo

Grouping of World War I medals belonging to General Achille D'Havet; from left to right: The Military Order of Savoy for Military Merit; Silver Medal for Military Valor, World War I action, dated and named; Same as the preceding medal, but for a different battle and date; Bronze Medal for Military Valor, Wrold War I action, dated and named; The War Merit Cross. Rudy D'Angelo

LUXEMBOURG

With ties to both Germany and the netherlands through their royal houses, medals from Luxembourg are both interesting and attractive; while presently not highly sought after by the collector, they do have a lot to offer for the future. All awards are finely designed and produced, showing to effect the best of the jeweler's trade.

Star, with Swords, of Second Class Commander of the Military Order of Merit of Adolph of Nassau.

Commander's Cross of the Order of Military Merit of Adolph of Nassau.

Star of the Grand Cross of
the Military Order of Merit
of Adolph of Nassau.

Star of the Grand Officer
of the Military Order of
Merit of Adolph of
Nassau.

Commander's Cross with
Crown of the Military
Order of Merit of Adolph
of Nassau.

Cross of Merit of the
Military Order of Merit of
Adolph of Nassau.

Cross of the Grand Cross
of the Order of the Oak
Crown.

Star of the Grand Cross of
the Order of the Oak
Crown.

Star of the Grand Officer
of the Order of the Oak
Crown

Knight's Cross of the
Order of the Oak Crown.

Silver Medal of Merit of
the Order of the Oak
Crown.

Gilt Medal of Merit of the
Order of the Oak Crown.

MONTENEGRO

A small, fiercely independent, mountainous nation on the Adriatic Sea, few awards were presented by this wretchedly poor kingdom in the short five years of its existence, or in the previous 57 years as a principality, prior to being absorbed into Yugoslavia at the end of World War I. Decorations and medals were often made in Vienna, while some appear to have been manufactured in Italy.

First Class Star of the Order of Danilo.

First Class Cross of the Order of Danilo.

NETHERLANDS

Due to the tumultuous imperial history of the Netherlands, the awards of this country reflect the expansion, the colonization and the world-wide spread of Dutch culture. Beautifully designed and produced, the orders and decorations are a delight to the collector, with their variety and interesting background.

Bottom center: Star of the Grand Cross of the Military Order of William.
Top: Grand Cross and sash of the Military Order of William.
Bottom left: Third Class Knight's Cross of the Military Order of William.
Bottom right: Fourth Class Knight's Cross of the Military Order of William.

Top: Star of the Grand Cross of the Order of Orange-Nassau.
Center: Star of the Grand Officer of the Order of Orange-Nssau.
Bottom left: Officer's Cross of the Order of Orange-Nassau.
Bottom right: Knight's Cross of the Order of Orange-Nassau.
Bottom center: Golden Medal of Honor of the Order of Orange-Nassau.

War Service Cross. John Edwards

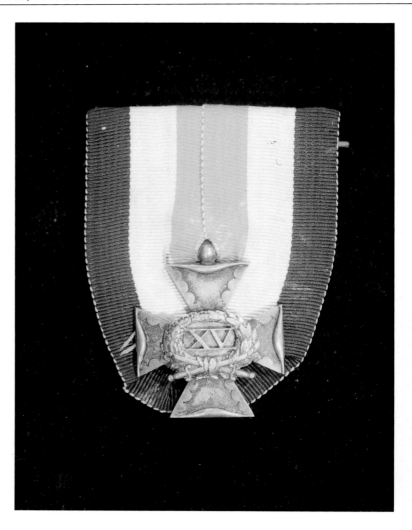

Officer's 15 Year Long Service Medal. Jeff Floyd

1830-1831 Metal Cross. Jeff Floyd

NORWAY

Only independent since the beginning of the century, Norway has not had a long history of military action. While quite impressive and very well made, the orders and decorations of this country are few in number. Collectors, however, are avid for those medals of World War II that do become available.

Left: First Class Knight's Cross of the Order of Saint Olaf.
Center: Commander's Cross of the Order of Saint Olaf.
Right: Knight's Cross, Military, of the Order of Saint Olaf.

The Medal of Saint Olaf.

Another view of theStar of the Grand Cross of the Order of Saint Olaf.

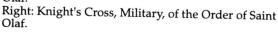

Reverse of the Star of the Grand Cross of the Order of Saint Olaf.

Right:
Top: Collar of the Order of Saint Olaf.
Bottom left: Star of the Grand Cross of the Order of Saint Olaf.
Bottom center: Grand Cross with Crown of the Grand Cross of the Order of Saint Olaf.
Bottom right: Star of the Commander of the Order of Saint Olaf.

POLAND

Poland has had a history of conquest from without since 1795, having been divided between Russia, Austria and Germany until freedom was obtained in 1918 at the end of World War I. Influences from all three of these countries are reflected in the awards of Poland; some of the Polish awards were actually incorporated into the awards of the conquering country, such as Russia. Medals of Poland will be found in differing states of quality, with many orders being quite rare. One will find much in the way of beauty in the medals of Poland.

Medal for participation in the Russo-Polish war of 1919-1920.

Cross of the Polish Soldiers from America, Russo-Polish War of 1919-1920. Awarded to American volunteers of the Kosciuszko Squadron, Polish Air Force.

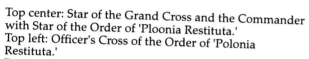

Top center: Star of the Grand Cross and the Commander with Star of the Order of 'Ploonia Restituta.'
Top left: Officer's Cross of the Order of 'Polonia Restituta.'
Bottom: Star of the Grand Cross of the Order 'Virtuti militari.'
Top right: Fourth Class Medal of the Order 'Virtuti Militari.'

Star of the Order of the White Eagle, 1922.

Badge of the Order of the White Eagle, 1922.

PORTUGAL

Among the oldest countries issuing orders and decorations, Portugal's older pieces are beautifully done and are much sought after by collectors; those pieces produced in the last hundred years pale by comparison. Awards by the Republic are not eagerly collected, and therefore the values are reasonable. In any case, the awards reflect the jeweler's art over the years.

Grand Cross Badge and Sash of the Order of Aviz.

Knight's Cross of the Imperial Order.

Another view of the Grand Cross of the Order of the Tower and the Sword.

Center right: Knight's Cross of the Order of Aviz, on a breast ribbon.
Top left & right: Collar of the Order of the Twoer and the Sword.
Center cen ter: Badge of the Grand Cross of the Order of the Tower and the Sword.
Bottom left: Star of the Grand Cross and the Grand Officer of the Order of Christ.
Center left: Officer's Cross of the Order of Christ.
Bottom right: Star, Grand Cross and Grand Officer of the Order of Aviz.
Top center: Knight of the Order of the Tower and the Sword.

Star of the Grand Cross of the Order of the Tower and the Sword.

ROMANIA

In the short, turbulent history of Romania, the country has been heavily influenced by Germany and France, with Bucharest considered the Paris of Eastern Europe; the Romanians have always thought of their language as a romance language, closely allied with French in its roots. Joining with the Allies in World War I, the Romanians were also under the influence of the Germans prior to and during World War II. The German influence in awards may be seen by the number of classes and swords, while the French influence is reflected in the terminology and the use of rosettes. Earlier pieces were produced in Austria, while many nice pieces were done by French manufacturers, with many of the awards being quite impressive.

Star of the Order of the Crown, first type.

Grand Cross of the Order of the Crown.

Knight's Cross of the Order of the Crown.

Collar of the Order of Karol I.

Cased set of the Star and Grand Cross of the Order of Karol I.

Star of the Grand Cross of the Order of Karol I.

Close-up of the Grand Cross of the Order of Karol I.

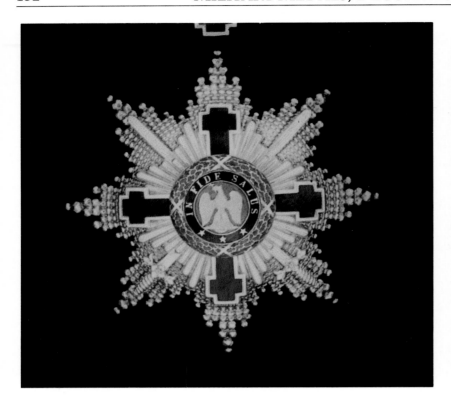

Star of the Grand Cross of the Order of the Star of Romania, with Swords.

Knight's Cross of the Order of the Star of Romania.

The Romanian Sanitation Medal.

Grand Cross of the Order of the Star of Romania, with Swords on the ring.

The Medal for Bravery and Loyalty, with Swords.

Third Class Medal for Steadfastness and Loyalty, with Swords.

1st Class Military Service Medal.

2nd Class Military Service Medal.

3rd Class Military Service Medal.

The Romanian Victory Medal for World War I.

Guards Regimental Breast
Badge, pre-World War I.
Ron Wolin

The 1877 Danube Cross. Jeff Floyd

The Carol I Jubilee Medal.
Jeff Floyd

A beautiful Romanian medal bar, from left to right: The Pelesch Castle Medal, 1938; Order of
the Crown, Officer, 2nd type with Swords; Order of the crown, knight, 1st type; 25 year Long
Service Decoration; World War I Commemorative Medal; World War I Victory Medal;
Centenary of King Carol I. Jeff Floyd

IMPERIAL RUSSIA

Russia had the facilities and the talent to produce some of the most beautiful medals to be found, comparing in quality with the finest produced in Austria, Switzerland, Germany or Great Britain. The enameling and the metal work in gold were second to none. It is therefore not surprising that the medals of Russia provide collectors with a fascinating and rewarding Venue in which to expand their search. The strong influence of religion in the Russian daily life is also prominently reflected in their awards, decorations and orders.

Star of the Order of the White Eagle.

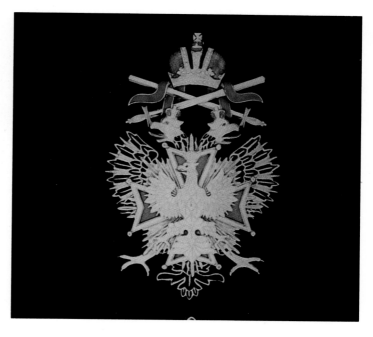

Badge of the Order of the White Eagle, with Swords.

Star of the Alexander Nevsky Order, 1814

Badge and Sash of the Alexander Nevsky Order, 1814.

Star of the Alexander Nevsky Order.

First Class Cross of the Alexander Nevsky Order, late war issue.

Star of the Order of Saint Andrew.

Badge and sash of the Order of Saint Andrew.

Star of the Grand Cross of the Order of Saint Stanislaus.

First Class Cross of the Order of Saint Stanislaus.

First Class Star of the Order of Saint Vladimir.

Star and Second Class Commander's Cross of the Order of Saint George.

First Class Star of the Order of Saint George.

Second Class Cross with Swords of the Order of Saint Vladimir.

First Class cross of the Order of Saint Anne.

A Russian grouping, from left to right: Fourth Class Cross of the Order of Saint George; The Order of Saint Anne, Third Class with Swords; The Order of Saint Stanislaus, Third Class with Swords.

SERBIA - YUGOSLAVIA

The basis for the Kingdom of Yugoslavia was the kingdom of Serbia, which, along with other territories including Montenegro, Bosnia and Croatia, made up the unified slavic state. Serbia, with the most longevity, had the greater number of orders and awards, many of which are quite lovely. The orders of Montenegro, while beautiful, were of short duration. Prior to World War I, most orders of Serbia and Montenegro were made by Austrian firms. Until recent times, the Order of Saint Sava has been awarded by the late King Peter. The awards of Serbia-Yugoslavia will reward the diligent collector with many pieces of unsurpassed beauty.

Star of the Order of the Star of Karageorg, founded by King Peter I in 1904; this order came in 4 classes.

Grand Cross of the Order of the Star of Karageorg.

159

First Class Star of the Order of Takova.

First Class Cross of the Order of Takova.

Knight's Cross of the Order of Takova. Jeff Floyd

Star of the Order of Saint Sava.

Right: Commander's Cross of the Order of Saint Sava.

Far right: Knight's Cross of the Order of Saint Sava.

Star of the Grand Cross with Swords of the Order of the White Eagle.

Commander's Badge with Swords of the Order of the White Eagle.

Reverse of the Knight's Badge of the Order of the White Eagle.

A grouping of the Obilitch Medal for Bravery, founded in 1889. It came in 2 classes, gold and silver, as well as in 2 sizes.

The Medal of King Peter I, in commemoration of the restoration of the Karageorgevitch dynasty.

Reverse of the Medal of King Peter I.

Commemorative Medal for Loyalty to the Fatherland (1915), or better known as the Medal of Albania, commemorating the retreat of Serbian forces through Albania in 1915.

Commander's Cross of the Crown of Yugoslavia.

Reverse of the Medal of Albania.

A grouping of medals, from left to right: the Medal of King Peter I; The Commemorative Medal for the Balkan War of 1912; The Commemorative Medal for the War of 1913; The Medal of Albania; The 1885-1886 War Medal.

SPAIN

The long, chaotic and religious history of Spain is well reflected in the country's orders, decorations and medals. Profusely distributed under the monarchy, this practice was even more greatly increased under the Franco regime. Due to the various civil wars and colonial adventures undertaken by Spain, a very wide range of selections is available to the collector —from rather crudely made campaign medals to fine pieces of jewel-like quality in other decorations and orders.

Breast Badge of the Yoke and Arrows, Spanish Falange.

Third Class Star for general service, of the Air Force Order of Merit.

Top left: Second Class Star for war service of the Military Order of Merit.
Top right: Third Class Star for general service of the Military Order of Merit.
Center left: First Class Cross for war of the Military Order of Merit.
Center right: First Class for general service of the Military Order of Merit.
Center center: Second Class Star for general service of the Naval Order of Merit.
Bottom 2 left: First Class Cross for war of the Naval Order of Merit.
Bottom 2 right: First Class Cross for general service of the Naval Order of Merit.
Bottom left: Frist Class Cross for war of the Air Order of Merit.
Bottom right: First Class Cross for general service of the Air Force Order of Merit.

164

Commander's Badge of the Order of Africa.

Grand Cross of the Order of Carlos III.

First Class Star of the Order of Carlos III.

Star of Military Justice, made in Cuba pre-1898. Note the Golden Fleece surrounding the shield.

1895-1898 Spanish-Philippine Medal

SWEDEN

Unfortunately for the collector, Sweden was a mighty power to be reckoned with prior to the time when it was fashionable to issue awards. In modern times, Sweden has not been at war with its neighbors, with the obvious result that there are relatively few military orders and awards. Made of silver and gold, those that do appear, however, are most beautiful in appearance and quality.

Star of the Royal Order of the Sword.

Top: Collar of the Royal Order of the Sword.
Bottom center: Star of the Commander of the Grand Cross of the Royal Order of the Sword.
Top center: Badge of the Commander of the Grand Cross of the Royal Order of the Sword.
Top left: First Class Kinght's Cross of the Royal Order of the Sword.
Bottom left: Kinght's Cross of the Royal Order of the Sword.
Top right: War Cross of the Royal Order of the Sword.
Bottom right: Medal of the Royal Order of the Sword.

TURKEY

Turkey was known as the Ottoman Empire until the advent of the Turkish Republic in 1921. The medals of the Ottoman Empire are a reflection of the decline of the Empire during the last 100 years. Many of the Turkish awards are readily recognizable because, due to their having been awarded to many German officers and men during the first World War, they are of unusual and unexpected design within a grouping of German medals. The medals produced during the war were often crudely made, while those of an earlier vintage are quite beautiful and, understandably most sought after by collectors.

Star of the Order of Osmania.

Star of the Grand Cross of the Order of Medjidjie.

Commander's Badge of the Order of Osmania.

Badge of the Order of Medjidjie, established 1852, and awarded as shown to German Officers in World War I.

From left to right, the Turkish War Medal, or 'Gallipoli' Star, as awarded to German officers and men who fought with the Turks in World War I; the Imtiaz Medal, also awarded as previously stated.

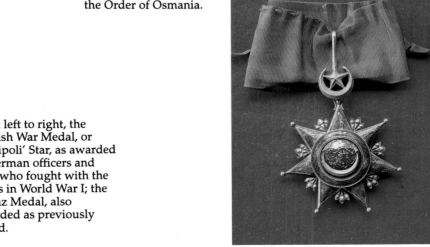

UNITED STATES

The United States is unique among nations in that there was a limited need for decorations, awards, badges, or medals until relatively late in the 19th century, when, after the Civil War, recognition of the role of the military assumed greater importance. With the advent of the Spanish American War, campaign medals for the various branches of the service began to proliferate. Only those medals officially recognized prior to World War II are shown here since the collector is less likely to have uncovered detailed information on many of these. In contrast, considerable reference material is already available for those awarded during World War II and subsequent U.S. actions and engagements.

The guild system of apprenticeship common to European countries renowned for their artisanship in fine jewelry design was the training ground for many immigrants who made their way to America and continued their trade, often through many generations. That pride of workmanship and attention to detail is evident in the U.S. medals that were later awarded to its valiant heroes.

Medals of Honor, on the left, the Army Medal of Honor, from 1862-1896, and on the right, the Navy Medal of Honor, 1862-1913.

Medals of Honor, on the left, the Army Medal of Honor, from 1896-1904; on the right, the Navy Medal of Honor, from 1913-1942.

Medals of Honor, on the left, the Army Medal of Honor, from 1904-1944; on the right, the Navy Medal of Honor, from 1919-1942.

The Distinguished Service Cross, awarded to Army personnel; ranked next to the Medal of Honor and awarded only for extraordinary heroism in combat.

U.S. Marine Corps Brevet Medal, established in 1921 for those marines who received brevet commissions for bravery. Only 20 medals were awarded.

Certificate of Merit, Army, 1905-1918. Replaced by the DSC.

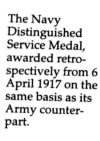

The Navy Distinguished Service Medal, awarded retrospectively from 6 April 1917 on the same basis as its Army counterpart.

The Navy Cross, originally authorized as the Navy's third highest decoration for acts of heroism in action and other distinguished services – in 1942, it became the Navy's second highest award, next to the Medal of Honor.

The Silver Star Medal, awarded to Army personnel in World War I for gallantry in action not warranting the award of the Distinguished Service Cross or the Medal of Honor.

The Army Distinguished Service Medal, the highest award for exceptionally meritorious service to the government in a duty of great responsibility.

The Distinguished Flying Cross, awarded for heroism or extraordinary achievement while participating in an aerial flight subsequent to 11 November 1918.

The Soldier's Medal, a reward for heroism during peacetime.

The Gold Lifesaving Medal, 1882-1949.

The large issue Silver Lifesaving Medal, as awarded from 1882-1949.

A copy of the original Badge of Merit (Purple Heart) established by George Washington in 1782. This was awarded only three times.

The Purple Heart, awarded for wounds received in action. This particular medal was awarded to 2nd Lt. William D. Ball for wounds received at the Meuse – Argonne in World War I.

The Army Good Conduct Medal.

The Navy Good Conduct Medal, First style, 1869-1884.

The Navy Good Conduct Medal.

The Marine Corps Good Conduct Medal, authorized in 1896.

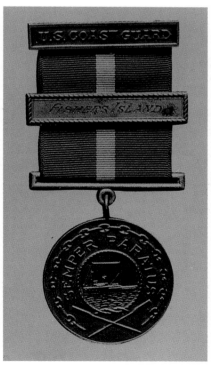

The Coast Guard Good Conduct Medal.

Army Civil War Campaign Medal.

Navy Civil War Campaign Medal.

The Indian Wars Medal, Army.

West Indies Naval Campaign Medal, or better known as the "Sampson" Medal.

The Manila Bay, or "Dewey" Medal, Navy and Marine Corps.

Spanish Campaign Medal - Army.

The Navy and Marine Corps West Indies Naval Campaign Medal for specially meritorious service other than in battle, awarded to Naval and Marine Corps personnel.

Army of Puerto Rico Occupation.

Spanish Campaign Medal
- Navy and Marine Corps.

China Relief Expedition
Medal - Army.

Philippine Campaign
Medal - Army.

Army of Cuba Occupation Medal.

Philippine Congressional
Medal.

China Relief Expedition Medal - Navy and Marine Corps.

Cuban Pacification Medal - Army.

Nicaraguan Campaign Medal.

Cuban Pacification Medal - Navy and Marine Corps.

First Haitian Campaign Medal with bar '1919-1920' for the Second Haitian Campaign.

Mexican Service Medal - Army.

Mexican Service Medal - Navy and Marine Corps.

Mexican Border Service Medal.

Dominican Campaign Medal, 1916.

Army of Occupation of Germany Medal.

Haitian Campaign Medal, 1919-1920, for the Navy and Marine Corps.

Second Nicaraguan Campaign Medal.

Yangtze Service Medal.

China Service Medal -
Navy and Marine Corps.

Marine Corps Expedition-
ary Medal.

Marine Corps Reserve Medal.

Navy Expeditionary Medal.

Another view of the
American Victory Medal,
with the bar
"Minesweeping."

American Victory Medal for World War I, illustrating 19 of
the bars possibly awarded to an individual or unit.
Apparently, no more than 6 bars were ever awarded. This
particular medal came from a museum, and is marked on
the edge "For Display Only."

The Peary Polar Expedition Medal, 1908-1909.

The Gold Byrd Antarctic Expedition Medal, 1928-1930, this medal also came in silve and bronze.

The 1933-1935 Antarctic Medal.

The 1939-1940 Antarctic Medal.

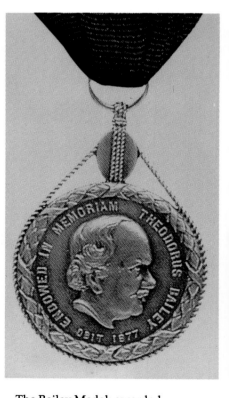

The Bailey Medal; awarded annually to a naval apprentice with an outstanding record in memory of Admiral Bailey (1805-1877.)

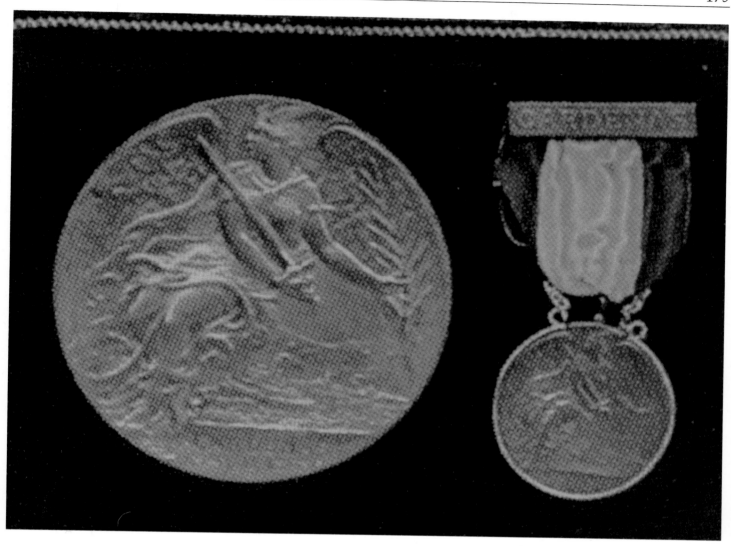

The Cardenas Medal of Honor; awarded to officers and men of the Revenue Cutter USRCS Hudson for gallantry during the Spanish American War.

The NC-4 Medal, awarded to Navy Commander John H. Towers and officers and crew members of Navy flying boat NC-4 who crossed the Atlantic in May 1919.

BIBLIOGRAPHY

Dorling, H. Taprell, *Ribbons and Medals*, Doubleday,Garden City, New York, 1974.

Deutschland-Katalog, *Orden & Ehrenzeichen, 1800-1945*, Jorg Nimmergut, Munich, Germany, 1977.

Falkenstien, Joseph von, *Imperial Austrian Medals and Decorations*, Mohler and Wilkinson, Sausalito, CA., 1972.

Henric's Oldenkott Senior & Co., *Die Orden und Ehrenzeichen der Deutschen Bundesstaaten im Weltkrieg 1914-1918*.

Hieronymussen,Paul, *Orders and Decorations of Europe in color*, the MacMillan Co., New York, 1970.

Kerrigan, Evans, *American War Medals and Decorations*, Viking Press, New York, 1964.

Mericka, Vaclav, *Orden und Auszeichnungen*, Svoboda, Prague, Czechoslovakia, 1966

Neville, D.G., *Medal Ribbons and Orders of Imperial Germany & Austria*, Balfour Publications,St. Ives, Huntingdon, Cambridgeshire, England, 1974.

Orden, Waldorf-Astoria GmbH, Munich, Germany, 1920.

Purves, Alec A., *The Medals Decorations & Orders of the Great War, 1914-1918.*,J.B.Hayward & Son, London, England, 1975.

Vernon, Sydney B., *Vernon's Collectors Guide to Orders, Medals & Decorations*, Sydney B. Vernon, Wildomar, CA., 1990.

Werlich, Robert, *Orders and Decorations of All Nations*, 2nd Edition, Quaker Press, Washington, D.C., 1974

*Fur Tapferkeit und Verdienst,*Schild Verlag, Munich, Germany.

VALUE GUIDE

Values vary immensely according to the condition of the piece, the location of the market, and the overall quality of the individual item. All of these factors make it impossible to create an accurate value listing, but we can offer a guide. These values reflect what one could realistically expect to pay at retail or auction. It is, however, only a guide, and the authors accept no responsibility for any gain or loss the reader may experience as a result of using this guide.

The lefthand number is the page number. The letters following it indicate the position of the photograph on the page: T=top, L=left, TL=top left, TC=top center, TR=top right, C=center, CL=center left, CR=center right, R=right, B=bottom, BL=bottom left, BC=bottom center, BR=bottom right. In photos where more than one object are identified, the values follow the order in the caption. The right hand numbers are the estimated values according to the following chart:

A - up to $100
B - $100 - $250
C - $250 - $500
D - $500 - $1000
E - $1000 - $2500

F - $2500 - $5000
G - $5000 - $7500
H - $7500 - $10000
I - in excess of $10000

Page	Pos	Val		Page	Pos	Val		Page	Pos	Val
8		C		24	BC	B		40	BR	A,A,A
9	L	B		24	BR	A		41	TL	I,D
10		F		25	T	B		41	TC	A,A
11	T	E		25	BL	A		41	TR	C
11	BL	D		25	BC	B		41	CL	D
11	BR	E		25	BR	A		41	C	D
12	TL	E		26	TL	A		41	BL	C
12	TR	E		26	TC	A		41	BL	C
12	BL	E		26	TR	A		41	BC	C
12	BR	G		26	BL	A		41	BC	A
13	T	A,A		26	BC	B		41	BR	A
13	B	A,A,A		26	BR	B		42	BL	F
14	TL	D		27	T	A		42	BR	I
14	TR	A		27	BL	A		43		F
14	B	A,A		27	BR	A		44	T	E
15	TL	A		28	CL	C		44	BL	A
15	TR	A		28	BR	C		44	BR	E
15	BL	A		29	T	B,B		45	TL	E
15	BR	C		29	BL	A		45	BL	A
16	TL	A		30	L	C		45	BR	B
16	TR	A		31	T	A,A,A		46	TL	A
16	BL	A		31	BL	A		46	TR	A
16	BR	A		31	BR	A		46	BL	A
17	TL	A		32	TL	A,A		46	BR	A
17	BR	A,A		32	BL	A		47	TL	A
18	T	A,A,A,A		33	T	A		47	TR	A
18	B	A,A,A,A		33	B	A		47	BL	A
19	T	A		34	L	A		47	BR	B
19	BL	B		34	CR	D		48	L	A
19	BR	A		34	BR	B		48	R	A
20	T	A,A		35	L	A		49	TL	A
20	B	B,B		35	R	A		49	TR	A
21	TL	A		36	L	A		49	BL	A
21	B	B		36	R	A		49	BR	A
22	CL	C		37	T	B		50	BL	I
22	BR	C		38	L	I,I,I,E,I		50	BR	D
23	TL	B		38	R	D,D,D,D,A		51	TL	D
23	TC	D		39	T	A		51	B	D
23	TR	B		39	BL	D		52	TL	C
23	BL	C		39	BR	D		52	BL	G
23	BR	C		40	TL	E		52	BR	G
24	TL	C		40	TC	D		53	TL	G
24	TR	B		40	TR	B		53	B	I
24	C	A		40	BL	I		54	TL	E
24	BL	A		40	BC	I		54	TR	F

54	B	I	75	B	B	91	TR	A
55	TL	D	76	TL	I	91	BL	A
55	TR	A	76	TR	F	91	BR	A,A
55	BL	I	76	BL	F	92	TL	I
56	TL	F	76	BR	I	92	TR	F
56	B	F	77	TL	F	92	BL	I
57	TL	G	77	TR	E	92	BC	G
57	BL	F	77	BL	F	92	BR	E
57	BR	E	77	BR	I	93	TL	F
58	TL	E	78	TL	F	93	TC	E
58	BL	E	78	TC	F	93	TR	F
59	TL	E	78	BL	E	93	BL	E
59	BL	E	78	BC	B	93	BC	F
59	BR	E	78	BR	B	93	BR	E
60	TL	E	79	TL	I	94	TL	D,C
60	TR	E	79	TR	F	94	TC	B
60	BR	A	79	BL	I	94	TR	F
61	T	C	80	TL	G	94	BL	I
61	CR	A	80	TR	E	94	BC	E
61	BL	B	80	C	F	94	BR	A
62	TL	E	80	BL	E	95	TL	A
62	TR	D	80	BR	B	95	TR	A
62	BL	E,B	81	TL	E	95	BL	A
62	BR	C	81	TR	F	95	BR	A
63	TL	A	81	BL	A,A	96	TL	G
63	TR	A	81	BR	B	96	TC	D
63	BL	E	82	TL	E	96	TR	E
63	BR	H	82	TC	C	96	CL	E
64	TL	I	82	BL	C	96	BC	E
64	TR	I	82	BC	A	96	BR	F
64	B	I	82	BR	A	97	TL	F
65	TL	D	83	TL	A	97	TC	E
65	BL	F	83	TR	A	97	TR	E
65	BR	B	83	C	A	97	BL	E
66	TL	C,C	83	BL	A	97	BC	D
66	BL	E	83	BR	A	97	BR	D
66	BC	C	84	TL	E	98	TL	D
67	TL	C	84	C	F	98	TC	E
67	TR	D	84	BL	I	98	TR	E
67	BL	F	84	BC	E	98	BL	E
67	BR	E	84	BR	E	98	BC	D
68	TL	Too rare to value	85	TL	A	98	BR	D
68	TR	A	85	TR	E	99	TL	C
68	BL	I	85	CL	E	99	TR	A
68	BR	A,A	85	C	E	99	BL	A
69	TL	B	85	CR	D	99	BR	B
69	TR	A,A	85	B	E	100	TL	G
69	CR	A	86	TL	D	100	TC	E
69	BL	A	86	TR	D	100	TR	F
69	BR	C	86	BL	D	100	BL	E
70	TL	A	86	BC	C	100	BC	E
70	TC	A	86	BR	A	100	BR	D
70	TR	A	87	TL	A	101	TL	D
70	BL	A,A	87	TC	A	101	TC	C
70	BR	A	87	TR	A	101	TR	B
71	TL	D	87	BL	A	101	BL	B
71	TR	A,A	87	BR	A,A	101	BC	A
71	BL	A,A	88	TL	E	101	BR	A
71	BC	A	88	TC	E	102	TL	E
71	BR	A	88	TR	F	102	TC	E
72	T	A,A,A	88	BL	I	102	TR	E
72	C	A,A,A	88	BR	D	102	BL	D
72	B	A,A,A	89	TL	E	102	BC	D
73	T	A	89	TR	E	102	BR	C
73	BL	A	89	CR	F	103	TL	B
73	BC	B	89	BL	E	103	TR	B
73	BR	A	89	BC	D	103	BL	D
74	TL	C	90	TL	E	103	BR	B
74	TR	A	90	TC	H	104	TL	I
74	BL	A	90	TR	C	104	TR	D
74	BC	A	90	BL	A	104	BL	E
74	BR	A	90	BC	A	104	BC	E
75	TL	A	90	BR	B	104	BR	E
75	TR	A	91	TL	C	105	TL	E

105	TR	C
105	B	A,A
106	TL	F
106	TR	D
106	BL	E
106	BR	E
107	TL	E
107	BL	A
107	BR	B
108	TL	I
108	TR	E
108	CR	E
108	BL	C
108	BR	B
109	TL	A
109	TR	A
109	BL	B
109	BR	E
110	TL	C
111	TL	I
111	TR	E
111	BL	E
111	BC	C
111	BR	A
112	TL	E
112	TC	D
112	TR	B
112	BL	B
112	BR	A
113	CL	A
113	TR	C
113	BR	E
114	TL	E
114	TC	E
114	TR	A
114	BL	C
114	BC	D
114	BR	A
115	TL	F
115	TC	E
115	TR	A
115	BL	A
115	BC	B
115	BR	B
116	TL	F
116	TC	E
116	TR	F
116	BL	B
116	BC	A
116	BR	A
117	T	A,A,A
117	B	B
118	B	D
119	TL	I,I
119	TC	G
119	TR	G
119	BL	I
119	BR	D
120	TL	D
120	TC	E
120	TR	E
120	BL	E
120	BR	A
121	TL	I
121	TC	D
121	TR	H
121	BL	D
121	BC	D
121	BR	D
122	L	C
122	R	A,A
123	TL	C
123	TR	C,C,B,B
123	BL	A
123	BR	A
124		F
125	TL	E
125	TR	A
125	BL	A
125	BR	B
126	TL	A
126	TR	A
126	BL	A
126	BR	A
127	TL	A
127	TR	A
127	B	A
128	BL	D
128	BR	E
129	TL	A
129	CR	A
129	BL	A
130	TL	D
130	TC	C
130	TR	A
130	CL	D
130	BL	A
130	BR	A
131	TL	A
131	TR	A,A
131	CR	A,A
131	BL	A
131	BR	A,B
132	TL	A
132	TC	A
132	TR	A
132	BL	A
132	BC	A
132	BR	A
133	TL	A
133	TC	A
133	TR	A
133	BL	B
133	BC	A
133	BR	B
134	TL	A
134	TC	A
134	TR	A
134	BL	B
134	BC	A
134	BR	A
135	TL	A
135	TC	A,A
135	TR	A
135	BL	A
135	BC	A
135	BR	A,A
136	TL	A
136	TR	A
136	C	C
137	TL	A
137	TR	A
137	B	A,A,A,A
138	TL	A,A,A,A
138	TR	A
138	BL	A
138	BR	A,A,A,A
139	T	A,A,A,A
139	B	C
140	L	E
140	R	E
141	TL	E
141	TC	E
141	TR	E
141	CL	B
141	C	C
141	CR	C
141	BL	B
141	BC	A
141	BC	A
141	BR	A
142	CL	D
142	BR	D
143	L	E,E,A,A
143	TR	C
143	BR	C,B,A,A
144	TL	A
144	TR	A
144	B	A
145	TL	D,D,A
145	TC	A
145	BR	G,D,E,D
146	L	A
146	R	A
147	TL	C,A,D,A
147	TR	D
147	BR	E
148	L	C
148	R	A
149	TL	A,I,C,C,A,B,A
149	TR	C
149	BR	C
150	CL	B
150	CR	A
150	BC	B
151	TL	D
151	TR	F
151	BL	E
151	BR	E
152	TL	C
152	TR	A
152	BL	C
152	BR	A
153	TL	A
153	TC	A
153	TR	A
153	BL	A
153	BC	A
153	BR	A
154	TL	B
154	TR	A
154	BL	A
154	BR	C
155	L	F
155	R	H
156	TL	F
156	TR	G
156	BL	C
156	BR	G
157	TL	C
157	TR	H
157	BL	D
157	BR	E
158	TL	E
158	TR	I
158	CL	E
158	C	I,I
158	CR	E
158	BR	E,D,D
159	L	D
159	R	D
160	TL	D
160	TR	D
160	CR	B
160	BL	C
160	BC	B
160	BR	B
161	TL	D
161	CR	D
162	TL	B,A,B,A
162	BL	A
163	TL	B

No.	Code	Value	No.	Code	Value	No.	Code	Value
163	TC	B	169	BC	A	174	TL	D
163	B	A,A,A,B,A	169	BR	A	174	TC	A
164	TL	A	170	TL	A	174	TR	A
164	TC	A	170	TC	A	174	BL	C
164	R	B,C,A,A,B,A, A,A,A	170	TR	H	174	BC	E
165	TL	C	170	BL	E	174	BR	A
165	TC	C	170	BC	I	175	TL	B
165	TR	B	170	BR	A	175	TC	A
165	BL	B	171	TL	A	175	TR	C
165	BR	A	171	TC	E	175	BL	A
166	TL	C	171	TR	A	175	BC	A
166	R	F,D,E,B,B,B,B	171	BL	A	175	BR	A
167	CL	B	171	BC	B	176	TL	A
167	C	C	171	BR	C	176	TC	A
167	CR	C	172	TL	C	176	TR	A
167	BL	A,A	172	TC	B	176	BL	A
167	BR	B	172	TR	D	176	BC	A
168	BL	G,H	172	BL	E	176	BR	B
168	BC	G,G	172	BC	F	177		D
168	BR	F,I	172	BR	A	178	TL	I
169	TL	I	173	TL	D	178	TR	I
169	TC	D	173	TC	C	178	BL	I
169	TR	A	173	TR	B	178	BC	D
169	CR	A	173	C	A	178	BR	I
169	BL	B	173	BL	A	179	T	I
			173	BR	A	179	BR	I